OPTIONS TRADING

USES MONETARY PSYCHOLOGY TO INVEST IN STOCKS, BINARIES AND THE ETF MARKET AS A PASSIVE INCOME FOR THE FUTURE. TECHNICAL ANALYSIS FOR FINANCIAL LEVERAGE AND RISK MANAGEMENT.

Gianni Bond

INTRODUCTION 3

CHAPTER 1 — WHAT IS THE TRADING 6

CHAPTER 2 — MINDSET FOR TRADER 17

CHAPTER 3 — TRADING SOFTWARE AND OPERATING TOOLS 29

CHAPTER 4 — STOCKS MARKET BASICS 36

CHAPTER 5 — TYPES OF OPTIONS 47

CHAPTER 6 — TRADING STRATEGIES 53

CHAPTER 7 — BINARY OPTIONS: WHAT THEY ARE AND HOW TO USE THEM 68

CHAPTER 8 — TECHNICAL ANALYSIS AND ITS BASICS 79

CHAPTER 9 — PRINCING AND VOLATILITY STRATEGIES 91

BONUS CHAPTER : — THINK ABOUT CHOOSING A BROKER 100

CONCLUSION 105

Introduction

An option is basically an agreement on the underlying shares of stock. It's an agreement to exchange shares at a fixed price over a certain timeframe (they can be bought or sold). The first thing that you should understand about options is the following. Why would someone get involved with the options trading in the first place? Most people come to options trading with the hope of earning profits from trading the options themselves. And that's probably going to describe most readers of this book. But to truly understand what you're doing, you need to understand why options exist, to begin with.

There are probably three main reasons that options on stocks exist. The first reason is that it allows people that have shares of stock to earn money from their investment in the form of regular income. So, it can be an alternative to dividend income or even enhance dividend income. As we are going to see you later, if you own a minimum of 100 shares of some stock, this is a possibility. Then you can sell options against the stock and earn income from that over time intervals lasting from a week to a month, generally speaking. Obviously, such a move entails some risk, but people will enter positions of that type when the relative risk is low.

The second reason that people get involved with options is that they offer insurance against a collapse of the stock. So, once again, an option involves being able to trade shares of the stock at a fixed price that is set at the time the contract is originated. One type of contract allows the buyer to purchase shares, the other allows the buyer to sell shares. This allows people who own large numbers of shares to purchase something that provides protection of their investment that would allow them to sell the shares at a fixed price, in the event that their stock was declining by huge amounts on the market. So, the concept is exactly like paying insurance premiums. It's unclear how many people actually use this in practice, but this is one of the reasons that options exist. The way this would work would be that you pay someone a premium to secure the right to sell them your stock at a fixed price over some time frame. Then if the share price drops well below that degree to price, you would still be able to sell your shares and avoid huge losses that were occurring on the market.

The third reason that I would give for the existence of options is that it provides a way for people to make arrangements to purchase shares of stock at the prices that they find attractive, which aren't necessarily available on the market. So, there is a degree of speculation here. But let's just say that a particular stock you are interested in is trading at $100 a share. Furthermore, let's assume that people are extremely bullish on the stock and they are expecting it to rise by a great deal in the coming weeks. Maybe, it's earnings season.

During earnings season, stock can move by huge amounts. But before the earnings call, nobody knows whether the stock is going to go up or down or by how much it's going to move. An options contract could allow someone to speculate and set up a situation where they could profit from a huge move upward without having to actually invest in the stock.

Chapter 1 - What is the Trading

If you have spent any time looking at the world of investing, you may have heard about options at one point or another. They are sometimes going to seem pretty overwhelming to think about, but if you know a few key points that come with them, options can be pretty easy to understand. Options can be seen as another class of assets, just like mutual funds, ETFs, bonds, and stocks. And when the investor properly uses them, they can offer you some unique advantages that trading with the other assets just can't. You can purchase options like most other asset classes, simply by using an investment account from a brokerage. You may want to do a bit of research with these ahead of time to ensure you find the right brokerage firm for your needs. Options can be a powerful tool because they are going to do some wonders when it comes to enhancing your portfolio.

Options can provide you with this advantage as the offer a source of additional income, greater protection and further leverage. Based on the situation, you will find some sort of options contract that can provide you with an adequate alternative. In turbulent times, options are a great means of protecting your portfolio against sharp and unexpected declines.

In addition to protecting some of your personal assets, options are sometimes used to generate a recurring income. And some investors will choose to use these in a more speculative purpose, such as wagering on the direction that a stock will take. Just like with any of the other choices that you make with investing, options will involve some risks and you must fully understand these and know how to avoid them as much as possible. This is why any time you want to start trading options with a broker, there is going to be some kind of disclaimer like the following to help you know about the risk with options: Options involve risks and are not suitable for everyone. Options trading can be speculative in nature and carry substantial risk of loss. Only invest in risk capital. Options are going to belong to a larger group of securities that are known as derivatives. This is a word that many investors are going to associate with excessive risk-taking. In the past, Warren Buffett has even referred to these derivatives as a weapon of mass destruction when it comes to the stock market.

While there is some truth to this assertion, particularly when it comes to the irresponsible use of derivatives, the fact is that most derivatives are a good way for smaller investors to make some tidy profits. However, it is important to be aware that a derivative is a financial instrument that is based on the value on what is known as an "underlying asset". This means that the valuation of the contact will depend on the valuation of the asset that it is tied to. It should also be noted that you never actually own the asset when you take out an option until that option is exercised. By the same token, you never actually sell the asset until the option goes through.

Now, there are going to be a great deal of different securities that fall under this kind of label including calls, swaps, forwards, futures, and puts. If you already know how these options are going to work, and the right way to use them, you are going to have a huge advantage when trading in the market. Options are also nice because they will ensure the odds are put in your favor. If using options as a form of speculation doesn't seem to fit with the risks that you want to take or your trading choices, then you can also do options without any speculating. Even if you do decide to never work with options, it is important to understand how companies you invest in will use them. Some companies may use this in order to hedge their foreign exchange risk or give employees some stock ownership as well. And most of the multi-national corporations today are going to work with options in some form or another, and even as an individual investor you are able to use it to invest in many different securities.

There are two main types of options. The first is called a "call option". This option receives this name as it gives the bearer the right to buy. However, it does not constitute an obligation. What this means is that, if for whatever reason, the bearer chooses not to exercise their option, this is not penalized in any way. If the contract is exercised, then the bearer must go through with the purchase of the underlying security at the price agreed. This price is referred to as the "strike price".

The second type of option is called a "put option". This sort of option means that the bearer has the right to sell the underlying asset, but the contract itself does not represent an obligation to go through with the deal. This means that if the seller chooses to change their mind, they are free to do so as long as the provisions in the contract are met.

One way that you can think about a call option is like having a down payment for a future purpose. For instance, a potential homeowner sees that in an area of their town, there is a new development that is about to go up. This homeowner may decide that they want the right to purchase one of the homes in that area in the future, but they only want to be able to exercise that right once there are certain developments built around that area. Maybe they want to make sure that some schools are built there first or some other great amenities before they choose to purchase. These kinds of circumstances would then be able to affect the decision of the homeowner to purchase the home in that area. The potential homebuyer would benefit from the option of buying or not depending on whether the promised amenities show up or not and they can agree to purchase the home at a predetermined level.

In this example, the potential buyer could benefit greatly especially if and when prices for that property, or that sector, go up. Let's assume that both the seller and buyer agree at a sale price of $100,000. The buyer gets a call option for this price for a period of two months. At the maturity of the option, the buy has the right to purchase the property. In addition, the seller cannot sell the home to anyone else during that period even if the market value of the property goes up and other buyers offer more money. The seller can negotiate but cannot make a deal unless the option is exercised or declined.

If after the two-month period the option is exercised, the buyer goes through with the deal paying the $100,000 strike price. The buyer can make a great deal of money if the valuation of the property increases. For instance, if the valuation goes up to $125,000, the buyer can then turn around and resell at the higher price. The option also protects the buyer in case the price of the property falls. For instance, if they valuation falls from $100,000 to $80,000, the buyer has the option to decline. This can save the buyer from losing on the deal. The seller, of course, misses out on the sale and would have to figure out what to do with the property moving forward.

This is why options are seen as insurance policies. They can protect investors from purchasing assets which may suddenly decline in value, or lock in the price of an asset which is expected to go up at some point. If the buyer, or seller, decide no to go through with the option, they only lose the underwriting fee that goes along with the option itself. When you think about it, it's a small price to pay considering the potential losses that you could face especially in a volatile market.

What if, instead of a home, your asset was a stock or another investment vehicle. This is what is going to happen when we look at options trading and doing a put option. If you have an S&P 500 index portfolio, you have a choice to purchase one of these put options. An investor may choose to do this if they fear that a bear market is going to happen soon, and they refuse to lose more than ten percent of their long position in the portfolio. If the S&P 500 is currently trading at $2500, the trader is able to purchase a put option that provides them with the right to sell that index at $2250 at any point during a certain expiration date, such as within a few years. Then, if in six months or twelve months or another time period in that two years, the market ends up crashing by twenty percent, which is 500 points on the index, the trader has made 250 points by being able to still sell the index at $2250 when it is trading at $2000. This is a great option in order to help the trader only lose ten percent on their portfolio, even if the market goes down by twenty percent, or even more.

Of course, acquiring an option is not free. There is an implicit cost that comes with all options. This cost is a fee that is charged by the underwriter of the contract. This fee is charged to cover the expenses that the underwriter incurs when drafting the option.

The underwriter is an independent third party that looks to establish a neutral playing ground. None of the stakeholders in the contract may underwrite it (the buy or seller) as this would be deemed a conflict of interest. In this regard, the individual who takes out the option, regardless of its nature, must cover this fee. The fee is called a premium and may be subject to negotiation. For instance, both parties may agree to split the cost of the premium in case the option is exercised. Otherwise, the bearer would have to cover the cost.

Another important aspect pertaining to options contracts is the expiration date on the contract itself. These dates can vary according to the deal reached by both parties. If no action is taken by the date of maturity in the contract, the contract will be automatically exercised. This is done through computerized trading, meaning that the software will immediately carry out the contract when its maturity date is reached. So, if the bearer chooses not to exercise the option, they would have to do so before the date of maturity is reached on the instrument.

However, if you find that your option still has value when it reaches the expiration, then generally the broker is going to exercise the option automatically for you. In the put example that we had before, the S&P 500 fell to zero when it got to the expiration. But even with the fall, the 2250 put is still going to be worth 2250. At expiration, the put option that you purchased would settle for the cash value, which caused a large gain on the hedge. But, if the S&P 500 ended up at 3000 by the expiration date, then 2250 put that you have seen as worthless. Second, the one thing that you will really like about options is the limited amount of risk that you take on with them. At the most, you are only going to lose the premium that you paid in on the asset or the contract. If things go well, you get a good deal and make a profit. If things go poorly, then all you will lose is the amount that you invested in the beginning.

It should be noted that when you take out an options contract, you are really making a deal to purchase the asset which is pegged to the contract. This is why it is not recommended to take out options without first studying the asset and understanding the price dynamics behind it. As such, understanding the price dynamics will enable you to get a keen notion of its movements. This will allow you to estimate where the movements will go with the asset in question. As a result, you'll be able to make money the vast majority of trades your engage in.

Also, you can choose to work with other derivatives, commodities, foreign currencies, and bonds in order to get started with options trading. Buying and selling calls and puts: And before we end this chapter, it is important to know the cardinal coordinates that come with options and options trading to help you make smart decisions with your trading.

These will include: When you purchase the underlying asset, it is going to give you a long position. When you purchase a call option, it will give you a potential long position in the underlying stock. When you decide to short sell the stock, this means that you are going to have a short position instead. But if you sell either an uncovered or a naked call, it is going to give you a potential short position on that underlying stock to deal with. When you purchase a put option, it is going to give you a potential short position on that underlying asset. If you sell an unmarried or naked put, it helps you to gain a potential long position on that underlying stock. If you can keep these four scenarios separate, you will find that your investment is easier to work with overall.

One of the most important aspects to consider when dealing with options is that options are used to hedge risk. Since risk in an inherent part of trading, it is virtually impossible to ascertain the exact movements of stock markets. Therefore, options enable you to manage risk by setting a position in which you are able to protect yourself against wild swings. These swings receive the name of "volatility". So, the more volatility there is in the market, the harder it will be for you to predict where movements will take your securities. In the end, an option can automatically sell stocks at specific price points or buy them up when prices dip to a certain level. In the end, investing is about understanding and managing risk. This is why it's vital for you to become familiar with options as they can be the ticket to saving your portfolio from ruin should markets turn on a dime.

However, there is on word of caution: when you engage in computerized trading (either on your part or by your broker) you really need to keep your eye on the ball. Falling asleep on the wheel can lead to deals automatically being triggered. Therefore, you may find that a deal will go through even after you have changed your mind. So, tracking your positions is pivotal in avoiding any inadvertent deals which may cause you to miss out on important opportunities.

Chapter 2 - Mindset for Trader

Trading psychology is the mental state and emotions that determine the success or failure of trading options. It represents the aspect of your behavior that dictates the decisions you make when faced with a trade. The psychology is vital to any trade and can be compared to experience, knowledge, and skills in determining your success as a trader.

When you decide to start options trading, you need to grasp the concept of risk-taking and discipline that determine the implementation of any trade.

The two most common emotions are greed and fear, while others are regret and hope.

The Basics of Trading Psychology

We associate trading psychology to some behaviors and emotions that are often the triggers for catalysts for decisions. The most common emotions that every trader will come across is fear and greed.

Fear

At any given time, fear represents one of the worst kinds of emotions that you can have. Check in your newspaper one day, and you read about a steep selloff, and the next thing is trying to rack your brain about what to do next even if it isn't the right action at that time.

Many investors think that they know what will happen in the next few days, which makes them have a lot of confidence in the outcome of the trade. This leads to investors getting into the trade at a level that is too high or too low, which in turn makes them react emotionally.

As the trader puts a lot of hope on the single trade, the level of fear tends to increase, and hesitation and caution kick in.

Fear is part of every trader, but skilled traders have the capacity to manage the fear. There are various types of fears that you will experience, let us look at a few of them:

The Fear to Lose

Have you ever entered a trade and all you could think about is losing? The fear of losing makes it hard for you to execute the perfect strategy or enter or exit a strategy at the right time.

As a trader, you know that you need to make timely decisions when the strategy signals you to take one. When you have fear guiding you, the level of confidence drops, and you don't have the ability to execute the strategy the right way, at the right time. When a strategy fails, you lose trust in your abilities as well as strategy.

When you lose trust in many of the strategies, you end up with analysis paralysis, whereby you don't have the capacity to pull the trigger on any decision that you make. Making a move becomes a huge challenge.

When you cannot pull the trigger, all you can think about is staying away from the pain of losing, while you need to move towards gains.

No trader likes to lose, but it is a fact that even the best traders will make losses once in a while. The key is for them to make more profitable trades that allow them to stay in the game.

When you worry too much, you end up being distracted from your execution process, and instead, you focus on the results.

To reduce the fear in trading, you need to accept losses. The probability of losing or making a profit is 50/50, and you need to accept this fact and accept a trade, whether it is a sell or a buy signal.

The Fear of a Positive Trend Going Negative (and Vice Versa)

Many traders choose to go for quick profits and then leave the losses to run down. Many traders want to convince themselves that they have made some money for the day, so they tend to go for a quick profit so that they have the winning feeling.

So, what should you do instead? You need to stick with the trend. When you notice a trend is starting, it is good to stay with the trend until you have a signal that the trend is about to reverse. It is only then that you exit this position.

To understand this concept, you need to consider the history of the market. History is good at pointing out that times change, and trends can go either way. Remember that no one knows the exact time the trend will start or end; all you need to do is wait upon the signal.

The Fear of Missing Out

For every trade, you have people that doubt the capacity of the trade to go through. After you place the trade, you will be faced with many skeptics that will doubt the whole procedure and leave you wondering whether to exit the strategy or not.

This fear is also characterized by greed – because you aren't working on the premise of making a successful trade rather the fact that the security is rising without you having a piece of the pie.

This fear is usually based on information that there is a trend which you missed that you would have capitalized on.

This fear has a downside – you will forget about any potential risk associated with the trade and instead think that you have the capacity to make a profit because other people benefited from the action.

Fear of Being Wrong

Many traders put too much emphasis on being right that they forget that this is a business they should run the right way. They also forget that being successful is all about knowing the trend and how it affects their engagement.

When you follow the best timing strategy, you create many positive results over a certain time.

The uncanny desire to focus on always being right instead of focusing on making money is a great part of your ego, and to stay on the right path; you need to trade without your ego for once.

If you accommodate a perfectionist mentality when you get into trades, you will be after failure because you will experience a lot of losses as well. Perfectionists don't take losses the right way, and this translates into fear.

Ways to Overcome Fear in Trading

As you can see, it is obvious that fear can lead to losses. So, how can you avoid this fear and become successful?

- Learn

You need to find a way to get knowledge so that you have the basis for making decisions. When you know all there is to know about options, you know what to buy and when to sell, and learn which ones to watch. You are then more comfortable making the right decisions.

- Have Goals

What are your short term and long-term goals? Setting the right goals helps you to overcome fear. When you have goals, you have rules that dictate how you behave, even in times of fear. You also have a timeline for your journey.

- Envision the Bigger Picture

You always need to evaluate your choices at all times and see what you have gained or lost so far for taking some steps. Understanding the mistakes, you made gives you guidance to make better decisions in the future.

- Start Small

Many traders that subscribe to fear have lost a lot before. They put a lot of funds on the line and ended up losing, which in turn made them fear to place other trades. Begin with small sums so that you don't risk too much to put fear in you. Once you get more confident, you can invest larger sums so that you enjoy more profit.

- Use the Right Strategy

Having the right trading strategy makes it easy to execute your trades successfully. Make sure you look at various options trading strategies so that you know which one is ideal for your situation and skills.

Many strategies can help you succeed, but others might leave you confused. If you have a strategy that doesn't give you the returns you desire, then adjust it to suit your needs over time. Refine it till you are comfortable with its performance.

- Go Simple

When you have a strategy that is simple and straightforward, you will be less likely to lose confidence along the way because you know what to expect.

Additionally, the easier the strategy, the faster it will be to spot any issues.

- Don't Hesitate

At times you have to jump into the fray even if you aren't so comfortable with the way it works. Once you begin taking steps, you will learn more about the trade.

However, you need always to be prepared when taking any trade. The more prepared you are, the easier it will be for you to run successful trades.

- Don't Give Up

Things might not always go as you expect them to do. Remember that mistakes are there to give you lessons that will make you a better trader. When you lose, take time to identify the mistake you made and then correct it, then try again.

Greed

This refers to a selfish desire to get more money than you need from a trade. When the desire to get more than you can usually make takes over your decision-making process, you are looking at failure.

Greed is seen to be more detrimental than fear. Yes, fear can make you lose trades, but the good thing is that you get to preserve your capital. On the other hand, greed places you in a situation where you spend your capital faster than you return it. It pushes you to act when you shouldn't be acting at all.

The Danger of Being Greedy

When you are greedy, you end up acting irrationally. Irrational trading behavior can be overtrading, overleveraging, holding onto trades for too long, or chasing different markets.

The more greed you have, the more foolish you act. If you reach a point at which greed takes over from common sense, then you are overdoing it.

When you are greedy, you also end up risking way much more than you can handle and you end up with a loss. You also have unrealistic expectations from the market, which makes it seem as if you are after just money and nothing else.

When you are greedy, you also start trading prematurely without any knowledge of the options trading market.

When you are too greedy, your judgment is clouded, and you won't think about any negative consequences that might result when you make certain decisions.

Many traders that were too greedy ended up giving up after making this mistake in the initial trading phase.

How to Overcome Greed

Like any other endeavors in trading, you need a lot of efforts to overcome greed. It might not be easy because we are talking about human emotions here, but it is possible.

First, you have to know that every call you make won't be the right one at all times. There are times when you won't make the right move, and you will end up losing money. At times you will miss the perfect strategy altogether, and you won't move a step ahead.

Secondly, you have to agree that the market is way bigger than you. When you do this, you will accept and make mistakes in the process.

Hope

Hope is what keeps a trading expectation alive when it has reached reversal. Hope is usually factored in the mind of a trader that has placed a huge amount on a trade. Many traders also go for hope when they wish to recoup past losses. These traders are always hopeful that the next trade will be the best, and they end up placing more than they should on the trade.

This type of emotion is dangerous because the market doesn't care at all about your hopes and will take your money.

Regret

This is the feeling of disappointment or sadness over a trade that has been done, especially when it has resulted in a loss.

Focusing too much on missing on trade makes the trader not to move forward. After you learn the lessons after such a loss, you need to understand the mistakes you made then move ahead.

When you decide to let regret to rule your thinking, you start chasing markets with the hopes that you will end up making money on a position by doubling the entrance price.

Chapter 3 - Trading software and operating tools

First, there are generally two sites which are seen as the "best" for options trading: optionsXpress and TradeStation. Both of these have their own perks and their own reasons that you may decide to work through them.

OptionsXpress is a great place to start because they don't have an account minimum. They do ask a $12.95 commission on trades, and OptionsXpress only takes $1.25 for each contract. The fees can be a tad iffy depending upon your trade volume but generally, the fees are low compared to other options. The other great thing about options trading by way of optionsXpress is that they have a lot of features that you'd really come expecting. For example, they offer real time quotes, and also allow you to look at options chains. Even better, optionsXpress doesn't charge you extra at all for using these tools. Bear in mind that in the world of finance, platforms will always favor those who are able to move more shares and who trade more often. But with that said, as far as a cost effective options trading platform, OptionsXpress has you covered.

If you have a bit of money to invest, then you can go with TradeStation. TradeStation is generally ranked up there with optionsXpress in terms of really strong options trading platforms. And indeed, it's hard to find one much better than TradeStation. In exchange for a bit of a hefty account minimum, TradeStation offers you a huge amount of useful tools tucked right into their super handy platform. For example, you'll find yourself using features like automatic trade execution rather often. TradeStation is also built for people who understand technology such that they can develop, test, and sell their own trading strategies to other enterprising investors who may have an interest in such a thing. Of course, this doesn't mean necessarily that you have to use this utility, but it can certainly help you should you decide to use it. It has a high price tag with it, but it's very difficult to find a platform that is much better than TradeStation at what it's supposed to do: be a simple and straightforward platform which is highly extensible and super easy to build upon, should that be what you're wanting.

However, these can get rather convoluted. What if you just wanted simple, low-cost, and easy to understand, then it's hard to beat eOption. eOption is fantastic for low-capital investors who want the platform to just simply get out of their way and let them do their own thing. eOptions has an account minimum of $500, which isn't too much in terms of options trading, and their rates are extremely flat. They take a $3 trade commission, as well as fifteen cents for every contract that you decide to be involved with. If you haven't traded two times in the last year, or if you have less than ten thousand dollars in either your credit balances or your debit balances, you'll pay a fifty dollar fee for "account inactivity". They have an incredibly low margin rate, which means that their trading costs are low. The only place that you might get caught up is that they have a lot of data fees and platform fees. These can be a veritable cash rainbow of prices, and clock in at anywhere from $1 to $200 in a month, or possibly even more depending upon what all you're doing on the platform. As far as design and ease of use, there's not too much that's different from the others; there are an array of features that are available to you. Nothing particularly stand-out or amazing, but it certainly isn't a drab platform either. It's well-featured and if you just want a simple and low-cost platform other than optionsXpress, it's incredibly difficult to find something that will fill those shoes better than eOptions.

In terms of powerful trading platforms, there are two reigning kings: TD Ameritrade and OptionsHouse. Both have their own perks. Either one of these has one of the most high tech and fully loaded trading platforms that you can ask for, as well as with specifically useful features that you as the end user will find especially neat and handy.

TD Ameritrade doesn't have an account minimum and it takes a $9.99 trade commission. In addition, they have a promotion running which gives you six hundred dollars when you make a certain deposit. That can certainly be alluring in its own and give you a bit of extra capital to work with. TD Ameritrade operates on one of the most revered trading platforms in the business.

Known as thinkorswim, this platform is specifically created for active investors who are wanting the opportunity to get their hands on high quality tools and research, as well as who would like to try out different strategies or practice cost observation by analyzing the risks and benefits of certain interactions they could make on the marketplace. In addition, TD Ameritrade offers the Trade Architect service, based on the internet, as well as a Mobile Trader application for smartphones and other mobile devices. Should one use Trade Architect instead of thinkorswim, they'll find it lacking a bit in tools and services compared to the awe-inspiring thinkorswim, but nevertheless they'll still find an absolute wealth of complex features that they'll find useful regardless.

The other super impressive platform that one may be interested in is aligned with the OptionsHouse eTrade broker. They offer a huge array of tools which are usually relegated to financial professionals who make an absolute career out of carefully watching and analyzing the markets in different ways. In other words, they have a huge number of tools that will benefit the type who wants to be an active trader. OptionsHouse too has a decent trade commission: $4.95 per trade. They don't have a specific account minimum, and they offer a thousand dollars in free commissions when you make a certain deposit.

Lastly, there are a couple platforms which offer a great amount of utility in another way: the absolute wealth of market research and market data that they'll have available for free to any enterprising users who decide to use these services. In this category are Charles Schwab and Fidelity.

Fidelity has a $7.95 trade commission and a $2,500 account minimum. However, in return for this hefty minimum and hefty commission rate, you get access to one of the best stores of knowledge in the industry. They get a huge amount of research, bigger than almost anybody else, and they offer a lot of research from over twenty industry giants, such as McLean Capital Management. They make it super easy to access all of this and it also comes free with your account. They also offer an application for your mobile device which lets you access all of the research by way of your phone's built-in web browser. If you're looking for raw research, it's hard to do any better than using Fidelity Investments as your broker.

However, there is a tad more to knowledge than simply research, and Charles Schwab excels where Fidelity falls short. They have a $6.95 trade commission and a $1,000 account minimum. Additionally, they'll give you five hundred dollars in cash if you make a certain deposit, which once again could be useful for building up some expendable capital to use for your trading. In addition to a lot of raw research, Schwab has a tremendous amount of support for active traders, offering things such as trade assessment tools to allow you to see whether or not a trade you'd like to make is a bright idea. However, they also offer to you a ton of options market discourse by the analysts hired by Schwab, as well as seminars, both live and pre-recorded, both online and in-person. What's more is that the in person seminars are free to users of the service, because Schwab has a lot of branches throughout the country. What's more is that Schwab offers two top-notch platforms for stock trading. One is geared towards newer options traders, called StreetSmart, and the other is geared towards far more active traders, called StreetSmart Edge.

Really, knowing what options broker to go with is a matter of knowing yourself and your situation. Do you have a lot to spend on options trading? If you don't have a lot of investment capital, it's much better to start small and not invest too much in the first place, since your capital matters more to you by virtue of there being less of it. If you have a lot of investment capital and a basic idea of how to trade options, you'd be served well to go with one of the more research-heavy brokers geared at active traders. That too is a consideration in and of itself; do you want trading to be a significant part of your life? For example, do you want to do more with trading than just check the market every morning before work and night before bed? Do you want to spend a significant amount of time working on your portfolio and evaluating specific decisions to see which one would result in you making the biggest profit? If so, then you might find that you'd find yourself happier in the ones with a greater wealth of tools.

Chapter 4 - Stocks Market Basics

A stock is a form of security that suggests proportional ownership in a company. Stocks are acquired and sold predominantly on stock exchanges, however, there can be private arrangements as well. These exchanges/trades need to fit within government laws which are expected to shield investors from misleading practices. Stocks can be obtained from a large number of online platforms.

Businesses issue (offer) stock to raise capital. The holder of stock (a shareholder) has now acquired a portion of the company and share its profit and loss. Therefore, a shareholder is considered an owner of the company. Ownership is constrained by the amount of shares an individual owns in regard to the amount of shares the company is divided into. For example, if a company has 1,000 shares of stock and one individual owns 100 shares, that individual would receive 10% of the company's capital and profits.

Financial experts don't own companies as such; instead, they sell shares offered by companies. Under the law, there are different types of companies and some are viewed as independent because of how they have set up their businesses. Regardless of the type of company, ultimately, they must report costs, income, changes in structure, etc., or they can be sued. A business set up as an "independent," known as a sole proprietorship, suggests that the owner assumes all responsibilities and is liable for all financial aspects of the business. A business set up as a company of any sort means that the business is separate from its owners and the owners aren't personally responsible for the financial aspects of the business.

This separation is of extreme importance; it limits the commitment of both the company and the shareholder/owner. If the business comes up short, a judge may rule for the company to be liquidated – however, your very own assets will not come under threat. The court can't demand that you sell your shares, though the value of your shares will have fallen significantly.

Trading is the basic idea of exchanging one thing for another. In this regard it is buying or selling, where compensation is paid by a buyer to a seller. Trade can happen inside an economy among sellers and buyers. Overall, trade allows countries to develop markets for the exchange of goods and services that for the most part wouldn't have been available otherwise. It is the reason why an American purchaser can choose between a Japanese, German, or American conduit. Due to overall trade, the market contains progressively significant competition which makes it possible for buyers to get products and services at affordable costs.

In fiscal markets, trading implies the buying and selling of insurances, for instance, the purchase of stock on the New York Stock Exchange (NYSE).

Fundamentals of stock/securities exchange

The exchange of stocks and securities happen on platforms like the New York Stock Exchange and Nasdaq. Stocks are recorded on a specific exchange, which links buyers and sellers, allowing them to trade those stocks. The trade is tracked in the market and allows buyers to get company stocks at fair prices. The value of these stocks move – up or down – depending on many factors in the market. Investors are able to look at these factors and make a decision on whether or not they want to purchase these stocks.

A market record tracks the value of a stock, which either addresses the market with everything taken into account or a specific fragments of the market. You're likely going to hear most about the S&P 500, the Nasdaq composite and the Dow Jones Industrial Average in this regard.

Financial advisors use data to benchmark the value of their own portfolios and, some of the time, to shed light on their stock exchanging decisions. You can also put your assets into an entire portfolio based on the data available in the market.

Stock exchanging information

Most financial experts would be well-taught to build a portfolio with a variety of different financial assets. However, experts who prefer a greater degree of movement take more interest in stock exchanging. This type of investment incorporates the buying and selling of stocks.

The goal of people who trade in stock is to use market data and things happening in the market to either sell stock for a profit, or buy stocks at low prices to make a profit later. Some stock traders are occasional investors, which means they buy and sell every now and then. Others are serious investors, making as little as twelve exchanges for every month.

Financial experts who exchange stocks do wide research, as often as possible, devoting hours day by day tracking the market. They rely upon particular audits, using instruments to chart a stock's advancements attempting to find trading openings and examples. Various online middlemen offer stock exchanging information, including expert reports, stock research, and charting tools.

What is a bear market?

A bear market means stock prices are falling — limits move to 20% or more — based on data referenced previously.

Progressive financial experts may be alright with the term bear market. Profiting in the trade business will always far outlasts the typical bear market; which is why in a bear market, smart investors will hold their shares until the market recovers. This has been seen time and time again. The S&P 500, which holds around 500 of the greatest stocks in the U.S., has consistently maintained an average of around 7% consistently, when you factor in reinvested profits and varied growth. That suggests that if you invested $1,000 30 years ago, you could have around $7,600 today.

Stock market crash versus correction

A crash happens when the commercial value prices fall by 10% or more. It is an unexpected, incredibly sharp fall in stock prices; for example, in October 1987, when stocks dove 23% in a single day.

The stock market tends to be affected longer by crashes in the market and can last from two to nine years.

The criticalness of improvement

You can't avoid the possibility of bear markets or the economy crashing, or even losing money while trading. What you can do, however, is limit the effects these types of market will have on your investment by maintaining a diversified portfolio.

Diversification shields your portfolio from unavoidable market risks. If you dump a large portion of your cash into one means of investment, you're betting on growth that can rapidly turn to loss by a large number of factors.

To cushion risks, financial specialists expand by pooling different types of stocks together, offsetting the inevitable possibility that one stock will crash and your entire portfolio will be affected or you lose everything.

You can put together individual stocks and assets in a single portfolio. One recommendation: dedicate 10% or less of your portfolio to a few stocks you believe in each time you decide to invest.

Ways to invest

There are different ways for new investors to purchase stocks. If you need to pay very low fees, you will need to invest additional time making your own trades. If you wish to beat the market, however, you'll pay higher charges by getting someone to trade on your behalf. If you don't have the time or interest, you may need to make do with lower results.

Most stock purchasers get anxious when the market is doing well. Incredibly, this makes them purchase stocks when they are the most volatile. Obviously, business share that is not performing well triggers fear. That makes most investors sell when the costs are low.

Choosing what amount to invest is an individual decision. It depends upon your comfort with risk. It depends upon your ability and capacity to invest energy into getting some answers concerning the stock exchange.

Purchase Stocks Online

Purchasing stocks online costs the least, yet gives little encouragement. You are charged a set price, or a percent of your purchase, for every trade. It very well may be the least secure. It expects you to teach yourself altogether on the best way to invest. Consequently, it additionally takes the most time. It's a smart idea to check the top web based trading sites before you begin.

Investment Groups

Joining an investment group gives you more data at a sensible price. However, it takes a great deal of effort to meet with the other group members. They all have different degrees of expertise. You might be required to pool a portion of your assets into a group account before trading. Once more, it's a smart idea to examine the better investment groups before you begin.

Full-time Brokers

A full-time broker is costly on the grounds that you'll pay higher fees. Nevertheless, you get more data and assistance and that shields you from greed and fear. You should search around to choose a decent broker that you can trust. The Securities and Trade Commission shares helpful tips on the best ways to choose a broker.

Money Manager

Money managers select and purchase the stocks for you. You pay them a weighty charge, typically 1-2 percent of your complete portfolio. If the chief progresses admirably, it takes minimal amount of time. That is on the grounds that you can simply meet with them more than once per year. Ensure you realize how to choose a decent financial advisor.

File Fund

Otherwise called market traded assets, record assets can be a cheap and safe approach to benefit from stocks. They essentially track the stocks in a file. Models incorporate the MSCI developing business sector record. The reserve rises and falls alongside the file. There is no yearly cost. However, it's difficult to outflank the market along these lines since record supports just track the market. All things being equal, there are a great deal of valid justifications why you ought to put resources into a file funds.

Common Funds

Common assets are a generally more secure approach to benefit from stocks. The company supervisor will purchase a gathering of stocks for you. You don't possess the stock, yet a portion of the investment. Most assets have a yearly cost, between 0.5 percent to 3 percent. They guarantee to outflank the S&P 500, or other equivalent file reserves. For additional information, see 16 Best Tips on Mutual Fund Basics and Before You Buy a Mutual Fund.

Theories of stock investments

Theories of stock investments look like basic resources. Both of them pool all of their investors' dollars into one viably supervised hold. In any case, theories stock investments put assets into ensnared fiscal instruments known as subordinates. They guarantee to win the normal resources with these significantly used theories.

Theoretical stock investments are private companies, not open organizations. That suggests they aren't coordinated by the SEC. They are risky, yet various investors acknowledge this higher danger prompts a better yield.

Selling Your Stocks

As important as buying stocks is knowing when to sell them. Most financial experts buy when the stock exchange is rising and sell when it's falling. Regardless, a clever money marketer seeks after a strategy subject to their financial needs.

You should reliably watch out for the noteworthy market records. The three greatest U.S. records are the Dow Jones Industrial Average, the S&P 500, and the Nasdaq. In any case, don't solidify in case they enter a modification or a mishap. Those events don't prop up long.

If you don't have a great deal of time to deal for managing your stocks, you ought to think about a fixed portfolio. That recommends holding a reasonable blend of stocks, bonds, and commodities. The stocks will promise you benefit by market rises. The bonds and commodities shield you from downswings.

The particular blend provides you with flexibility. It relies on your cash related objectives. Perhaps you needn't sit around with the cash for a noteworthy timeframe, by then a higher blend of stocks will give a dynamically indisputable profit as time goes by. Perhaps you require the cash one year from now, you'll need more securities.

Rebalance your portfolio two or multiple times every year. It will hence guarantee you purchase low and sell high. For instance, if things progress enjoyably and stocks do poorly, your portfolio will have too high a level of commodities. To rebalance, you'll sell two or three commodities and get two or three stocks. That forces you to sell the commodities when costs are high and purchase the stocks when costs are low.

Chapter 5 - Types of Options

Options agreements come in two varieties. The first type of options contract is known as a call. A call option gives the buyer the possibility to buy some shares of stock at a fixed price. Usually, it's 100 shares. The agreed-upon value used to trade the shares is called the strike price. Every option comes with an expiration date, and so, if the buyer decides to purchase the shares, they must do so before the option expires. If the buyer decides to buy the shares, they are said to "exercise" the option. The party that sold to open the option, in that case, is said to be "assigned" if someone exercises the contract.

Options can be classified by the way they can be exercised. The possibilities are American-style or European-style. If you can exercise the option on any date, it's known as American style.

If the contract is a European style, the option can only be exercised on the day it expires. It's important to note that these terms don't necessarily mean that the option is trading in Europe or America. Although most options in America are American-style, there are some that are European style. Two examples are SPX and RUT. These are options used to follow the S & P 500 index and the Russell 2000 index. But the vast majority of options you're going to come across are going to be American style. If you sell options, this is something you need to be aware of. That means at any time that the option is an open position for you as a seller, you could be assigned.

The basic rule for a call option is that this is a bullish purchase. If you invest in a call option, your expectation is that's the price of the shares is going to rise. There are two ways that you can take advantage of this. The first way is to simply trade the option. As we will see later, small moves in the stock price translate into big moves for options prices. So, if the stock goes up in price, you can sell the option and make a profit.

The second way to profit would be to actually exercise the right to buy the shares. In that situation, you would buy the shares for the price per share given by the strike and then sell them on the open market to make a profit. In order to make money, the price on the market must rise to a level greater than the strike price added to the amount you paid to buy in the position.

So, if you purchased a $50 option for $1, meaning the strike price is $50, the price on the market would have to rise to $51 or higher to make exercising the option profitable.

The rule is that call options increase in price or value primarily when stock prices are rising. But, as we'll see, options are impacted by some other factors as well. But the general bet with a call option is earning profits when the underlying stock goes up in value.

Before we move on to consider the other major class of options, we need to make a clear distinction between selling and buying options. We can loosely use this language, but, actually, be applying it in very different contexts. First, let's consider simple options trading which is what most readers are going to be interested in. In this case, you enter a position by purchasing an option. So in market jargon, we would say that you are buying to open. So, in other words, you open your position by purchasing an option. If you buy to open an option you are never at risk of being assigned the shares of stock. So, you can sell the option and that carries no risk to you whatsoever. The only risk that you would face would be having to sell the option for a discount compared to what you paid to enter the position.

In contrast, you can also sell to open an options position. When you do that, you are at risk for the assignment with regard to the shares of stock. So that doesn't entail some risk but there are many reasons that people would choose to sell to open an options position. We will be exploring those later because selling to open a position can be an important part of options strategies. Also, you can sell to open positions in order to earn income from the premium.

The second type of option is called a put. A put option is a contract that allows the buyer to sell shares to the writer of the contract. This would be 100 of stock with a price given by the strike price. So, a put option has a strike price and expiration date just like a call option.

Put options actually increase in value if the market price of the stock declines. So if you buy a put, you are basically shorting the stock. If you intend to exercise the option, it would work in the following way. To use specific numbers, consider an example with the strike price of the option at $100 dollars per share. Then we will suppose that the company had a negative earnings call and the share price drop to $70 a share overnight. If you held the put option, you could buy the shares on the market at $70 a share. Then you can "exercise the option". That means you would sell the shares at the price of $100 a share because that was the strike price on the contract. So, you would make nearly a $30 profit per share by engaging in this trade. The profit would be given by the strike price minus the premium paid to buy the option minus the price you purchase the shares for on the market. So if we just imagine that the option cost $2 a share, the profit, in this case, would be $100 - $2 -$70 = $28 per share. Since there are 100 shares per option contract, that would mean a profit of $2800.

The general rule for put options, as we said, is that they increase in value when the share price drops. So many options traders are not looking to actually exercise the option. What they want to do is still hold the put option if there is a belief that the share price will decline, and then trade the put option on the market at a profit if the share price actually drops.

So, you might ask why would someone sell to open a put option? People sell put options in order to make money from the premiums. This can be done alone or in conjunction with a special option strategy that may involve both types of options. If you sell a put option, obviously you're hoping that the share price is not going to drop far enough to make it worth it to exercise. And in most circumstances, that's actually going to be the case. A higher risk here would be selling to open a put with a strike price that is near current market prices.

Chapter 6 - Trading strategies

Whether you are a beginner, average trader, or experienced options trader, there are strategies you need to use to make options work for you. When it comes to options trading, you do not need to be a genius to make it.

Many traders invest in options without the necessary information. This is one mistake that results in self-doubt and lack of confidence in the trade. People who do this often give up as soon as they start. With the right strategies in place, you can easily make income, secure your capital, and make the volatile nature of options to work in your favor.

Trading strategies help you reduce risks and maximize profits. If you do not have any strategy to follow, the business can become difficult and costly. Options strategies vary from simple ones to sophisticated ones but have one thing in common – they are all based on put and call operations. The payoffs do vary greatly, and before you settle on a strategy, be sure to understand how it works, the expected gain as well as if there are any risks involved. As a beginner, do not get overwhelmed with a large number of strategies available since you only need a few basic ones to get started. You can add more of these to your trading plan as you master the game.

This book focuses on some of the most popular basic strategies in the industry. Generally, options trading strategies can be divided into three categories - conservative long-term strategies, semi-conservative or short-term, also known as aggressive strategies.

• Conservative strategies are accomplished on a long-term basis. These allow you to build your capital in a slow but steady process. The benefit of such strategies is that they reduce the risk of losing your capital.

• Semi-conservative strategies consist of four to six trades per day. These are more aggressive than conservative strategies and involve more risk as well.

• Aggressive strategies allow numerous trades each day. These often result in higher risks and small profits.

With this in mind, you are able to define the type of strategies you need. If you are a day trader, then aggressive strategies will suit you better. Now, let us look at some of the strategies you need to understand to get started in options trading.

Strategies Related to Calls

The process of buying and selling of calls is one of the easiest in the options trading field. It is actually one of the popular and frequently used ways to get into options trading. This is because it allows you to own stock, using very little capital. Buying calls also presents you with a higher profit potential than purchasing stock. Some of the strategies you can exploit when buying calls are listed below.

Covered Calls

Covered calls entail setting up call options against your own stock. This strategy is not only popular in options trading but in other financial institutes that deal with stock as well. In this strategy, you only sell options to protect your stock from downward price movement and also increase your returns. Most investors do this any time there is a possibility of good gains on their stock. In most cases, they sell out-of-the-money calls, and once the price goes high, they trade the stock for a profit.

One advantage of this strategy is that you get to keep your stock at expiration if it falls below the strike price. If the stock goes above the strike price, you will sell the stock shares to the buyer at the strike price. Most investors use this strategy to generate profit at limited risks while retaining their stock.

The downside of covered calls is that you need at least 100 shares of stock to make the calls. The strategy is thus not beneficial for traders who wish to start small. Traders are also allowed to sell only one call option against 100 stock shares. This is called a covered call because, in the event that the stock price goes high, the call will be covered by the position of your stock.

You can consider using this strategy to make a profit if you already have the required stock and do not expect its cost to go high in the near future.

Bull Call Spread

In this strategy, you purchase calls continuously and at specific strike prices then sell these calls at higher strike prices. Normally, the calls have the same expiration time and are related to the same underlying security. Investors use this strategy when there is an expected rise in the cost of the underlying asset, especially during high volatile periods. When used correctly, it reduces the trader's upside and lowers the premium spent as compared to buying covered calls.

The strategy lowers the cost of a call option and defines a limit within which the investor can generate income. Here is the procedure of applying the bull call spread strategy:

• Select an asset that has the potential to appreciate in days, weeks or months

• Purchase a call option at a strike price that is higher than the current market price.

Specify the expiration date and make a payment for the premium.

- Sell a call option at a price that is higher than the strike price, but with the same expiration date as the initial call option. Do this simultaneously until the expiration time is reached.

By simultaneously selling call options, you will be able to receive a profit that will offset what you paid for the long or first call.

Since the strategy operates within limits, profits and losses are often constrained to certain amounts. This eliminates the possibility of losing all your stock to the trade. However, the disadvantage of this is that you cannot obtain any gain that is beyond the strike price of the sold call options.

Long Call

This strategy allows you to buy a call while expecting the prices to go beyond the strike price during expiration. One great advantage of this strategy is that if the prices go higher than the striking price, you can earn multiple times the initial premium since the trade has no upper limit. As the stock rises, the call keeps going higher. It is for this particular reason that long calls are common amongst traders who wish to make a profit from rising stock prices.

A disadvantage of this strategy is that if the expiration is reached and your stock is below the strike price, you may lose your entire premium. Therefore, use this strategy only when you are sure that the costs will keep rising until the option expires. If the stock rises only by a small percentage, you may lose part of the premium.

Long Call Butterfly Spread

This strategy combines the bull spread strategy and the bear spread strategy. These two strategies converge at the same strike price. Therefore, the long call butterfly strategy makes use of three strike prices. Just like the bull call spread, this strategy requires that you use call options derived from the same asset, and having the same expiration date.

Because the strategy allows you to sell two options at the same strike price, it is considered one of the low-price strategies that beginners can take advantage of. However, since it utilizes spreads of long and short calls, the chances of getting large profits are relatively slim. If the strike price is higher than the premium, the trade is considered to be bullish, and if it is lower than the premium, it is a bearish trade.

Short Call

In the short call strategy, you are required to sell your stock at a certain striking price assigned to the option. The main target of this strategy is for the call to expire worthlessly. The stock price must remain below the strike price for you to realize a profit. You risk losing your premium if the stock rises. Most traders only use this strategy when there is a high probability that the stock price will diminish. The more it rises, the more you lose money.

Related to this is the short call butterfly spread that involves selling one call option at low striking prices, buying two at-the-money call options, and then selling one out-of-the-money call option with a higher strike price. Profit is realized when the underlying stock's price rises over the higher striking price or goes below, the lower strike price during expiration.

Strategies Related to Puts

Buying of puts is one strategy you should use anytime you notice the market taking a direction that is against your call options. Traders buy puts whenever there is a possibility of the prices going down. Buying puts the opposite of buying calls. Here are some strategies related to the put option that may be of benefit.

Cash Secured Puts

This is the opposite of covered calls. This strategy requires you to sell puts against a liquid cash balance in your broker account. The only people who use this strategy are investors anticipating a decline in the stock price or those traders who wish to generate some profit from excess cash that is in their possession. Through selling puts against their cash, they are able to make some profit.

Generally, this strategy involves selling put options while saving enough cash on the side to purchase the underlying stock. It allows you to get stock options at discounted prices and sell them at a profit. The goal is to acquire the underlying stock at a price that is below the market price.

When the stock goes below the strike price, the put is assigned, and the trader allowed to buy the stock at the strike price. The process involves a lot of risks since the stock may decrease way below the strike price and this means that you may be required to purchase the shares at an amount that is above the current stock price. This comes as a loss to you, especially if the prices keep going down.

Married Put

This is where an investor buys stock and equivalent put options simultaneously. You can sell the put option at the strike price. Just like the covered call, each married put contract requires 100 shares. In this case, the trader is positive that the stock value will rise but uses a put option as insurance should the value go down.

The married put strategy is common in investors who have a vision of minimizing the downside risk of their stock. When an investor buys the shares and an option, he protects his stock from loss should a negative event occur and also makes some cash as the stock's value increases. However, if the stock does not go down, the investor loses the cash placed on the put option as a premium.

The married put has so many similarities with the covered call. It gets its name from combining or marrying a put option with the underlying stock. For every 100 shares, you are only allowed to buy one put option.

The maximum profit for this strategy is undefined. The more the stock appreciates, the higher the profits. One downside of this strategy lies in the cost of premiums. The put option increases in value as the stock value declines, and because of this, the trader loses the cost placed on the option. Such losses, however, cannot be compared to the value of the underlying stock which would have been saved in the process.

Long Put

Here, the trader purchases a put while expecting the prices to go below the strike price at expiration. It gives you the opportunity to multiply your initial investments in case the stock value falls at zero.

The long put has various similarities to the long call. The only difference is that you are expecting the prices to decline rather than go up. The upside of the long put is similar to that of the long call because the put option's value is capable of increasing in bounds. However, in this case, the stock should not go on the upside.

This strategy helps minimize the risk involved in shorting of stock. You must, however, note that if expiration is reached when the stock is above the strike price, the put option will be worthless and you will gain no profit.

The long-put strategy is ideal for use when you expect the stock price to fall before the expiration of the put option. The fall must be significant for you to return the premium paid; otherwise, you will end at a loss.

Short Put

Similar to the long put, the short put strategy is where you sell a put with the expectation that the price will rise above the strike price by the end of the trading period. In this strategy, you receive cash as a premium for selling a put. If the stock is below the strike price by expiration, you will be forced to purchase the underlying asset at the strike price.

The strategy is also known as the naked or uncovered put and gives an investor the right to purchase shares of an underlying stock when a put option buyer exercises the option.

For you to initiate a put option using this strategy, you have to be sure that the cost of an underlying asset will remain above the striking price. If the option expires worthless, you risk losing part of your initial investment. One downside of this strategy is that the profit is limited by the premium received, and there is a significant amount of risk involved. You should, therefore, use it only when they are positive that the stock will go up. You must also ensure that there is enough equity in your account to purchase the underlying stock should the put options work against your expectations.

Bear Put Spread

This is one of the best strategies for beginners since it involves short put spreads. The bear put spread can easily be applied to small and new trading accounts. It does not have any restrictions in terms of shares or premiums. It is also known as the short put spread and involves the selling of puts.

You can use this strategy when expecting the stock to remain at the same value or increase in price until the expiration date. If this happens, the option will expire worthlessly, and you will get your whole premium back.

To set up the bear put spread, start by selling a put option, then purchase another put option with a lower strike price than the one you sold. The option you buy should have the same value and expiration date as the one you sold. This makes your sold put more expensive than the one you bought, translating into some profit.

Unlike the long call, which returns multiple times of the investment, the short put spread can only give you a maximum return that is equal to your initial premium. This amount will be determined by the direction of the market. If the stock remains at the same level or goes beyond the strike price, you will get your premium back. If the stock decreases below the strike price, you will be forced to purchase the underlying stock at the strike price, and this result in loss.

Investors use this vertical spread strategy to make a profit from selling premiums to other investors who have bet against the stock prices going up. Because put sellers often have a certain number of shares to their name, they cannot get stuck when it comes to paying out on losses. In case you need to use this strategy, you must be careful that you do not sell your puts without first understanding the market. This is because stock prices may fall and claim all your premiums.

Other strategies combine put and call options to maximize profits. Some of them include the following.

Protective Collar

The protective collar strategy comprises of an out-of-the-money put option and a call option that run concurrently. This strategy is not so common in beginners, but if you master it correctly, you can lock some good profits from it. The combination of call and put options allows you to have downside protection to your stock while enjoying potential profits on the upside. It is the same us running the covered call and protective put strategies at the same time.

Investors use this strategy as another option to stop orders since they have the right to choose when to exercise their options. You can implement this strategy with little or no cost since the premium you get from the short call can be used to cancel out the cost of the long put. The strategy is called a collar because it helps you limit both downside and upside risk.

Chapter 7 - Binary options: what they are and how to use them

Binary options are similar to traditional options in many ways except that they ultimately boil down to a basic yes or no question. Instead of worrying about what exact price an underlying stock is going to have, a binary option only cares if it is going to be above one price at the time of its expiration. Traders then make their trades based on if they believe the answer is yes or no at which time it will be worth either $0 or $100. While it may seem simple on its face, it is important that you fully understand the ways in which binary options work, as well as the time frames and markets they work with. It is also important to understand the specific advantages and disadvantages that they have and which companies are legally allowed to offer binary options for trade.

If you are currently considering trading in binary options then it is also important to be aware that binary options trading outside of the US has a different structure. Also, when hedging or speculating, it is important to keep in mind that doing so is considered an exotic options trade so the rules are different still. Regardless, the price of a binary option is always going to be somewhere between $0 and $100, it is also going to come with a bid price as well as an ask price, just like any other type of option.

They are also a great way for those who are interested in day-trading but don't have the serious capital required to get off the ground, to ply their trade. Traditional stock day trading limits don't apply with binary options so you are allowed to start trading with just 1, $100 deposit. It is also important to keep in mind that binary options are a derivative created by its association with an underlying asset which means they don't give you ownership of that asset in any way. As such you would be unable to exercise them as a means of generating dividends or utilizing voting rights.

The benefits of picking binary options

Some of the benefits you will notice with using binary options instead of another investment includes:

The potential for a high return: this is a risky form of investing, but if you learn to read the market properly, you will find that it has a lot of potential for a lot of money to come to you. If you do well with this trading option, you could see a return on investment between 60 to 90 percent.

The risk is fixed: You will know right at the beginning how much money you stand to lose or to win depending on which way the prediction goes. This helps make it easier to decide on your choices. Other investments can end up being a lot of guesswork and if things go south, you can lose a lot more than you put into the whole thing. On the other hand, with binary options, you know exactly how much you stand to gain and lose right off the top.

You can even win after losing: Since you will find that the risks on these options are high, there are some brokers that offer a return on money that you invested if your predictions were wrong. This is not going to be the full amount but getting a small percentage of your money back can be encouraging compared to losing it all.

Easy trading: These are easier to trade on. Other options in the stock market make this hard, but the platforms for binary options help the investor trade without all the hassle. You can work with a live chat feature to do this or even with your broker if you have some questions. In addition, there are really only two options for most of your trading options so this makes things easier as well.

Rewards: The risk associated with any binary option is always going to cap out at the cost of the initial trade because the worst result for any option is for it to time out and be worth $0. The reward is also capped and based on the amount of the initial investment. As an example, if you purchase a $20 binary option then you are always going to make $100 at most, which means you will make $80 and have a 4:1 risk/reward ration which is better than you will find in most other situations most of the time.

This will only be in your benefit for a limited time, however, as gains will never increase pass $100 regardless of how much movement an underlying asset may have. The easiest way to mitigate this particular downside is to simply double down on options contracts from the start.

How to trade binary options

Binary options are currently traded on the Nadex exchange which was the first exchange created expressly to sell binary options in the United States. It offers market access as well as its own trading platform which always has access to the most recent binary options pricing.

It is also possible to trade options on the Chicago Board Options Exchange which can be accessed by those with an options trading approved brokerage account through more traditional means. When doing so, it is important to keep in mind that not all brokers are going to offer options trading which means that if this is a route you are considering going down you will need to plan accordingly and choose your broker with these services in mind.

Trading via Nadex costs 90 cents per trade with a maximum fee of $9 per transaction which means that lots greater than 10 are essentially free. The fee is not deducted from the trading account until the trade has expired and if the trade does not end profitably then there is no charge as well. Trading on the Chicago Board is subject to traditional brokerage fees.

Choosing the right market: There is nothing stopping you from trading across various asset classes at once when it comes to binary options and, indeed, Nadex allows trading across most of the major indices including the S&P 500, Nasdaq 100, Russell 2000 and the Dow 30. Available global indices include those from the UK, Germany, and Japan. Trades are also available for a variety of forex pairs including AUD/JPY, EUR/GBP, USD/CHF, GBP/JPY, USD/CAD, AUD/USD, EUR/JPY, USD/JPY, GBP/UDS, and EUR/USD.

Another popular option through Nadex is the commodity binary options which include crude oil, natural gas, gold, copper, silver, corn, and soybeans. There are also several options when it comes to trading based on a specific news event which means you can buy options on things like if the Federal Reserve is going to decide to decrease or increase the joblessness claims percentage or if the nonfarm payroll ends up beating its current estimates.

The Chicago Board offers a smaller selection of binary options overall, but those that it does offer are not available anywhere else. For example, it is only there where you can find binary options based on numerous interpretations of the S&P 500 or a volatility index based on its very own volatility index.

Binary option timeframes

Weekly trading: Weekly binary options are listings that provide the opportunity for trading in the short-term along with lots of opportunities to hedge the choices you do make. As you might infer from the name, weekly trading means working with options that expire in exactly one week with the standard being for them to be listed on Thursday and expire the next Friday. While this type of binary options trading has been around for quite some time, they were largely only used by investors who followed the cash indices. This exclusivity has changed in the past decade as the Chicago Board has started expanding the practice of this type of trading until now there are nearly 1,000 opportunities to do so each week.

Beyond just having a specific timeframe, weekly binary options are different than more traditional options in that they can only be purchased 21 days out of the month which is why they aren't listed as expiring in the monthly style. As such, in the week that monthly options are set to expire, they are technically classified as weekly options.

The biggest benefit with this type of binary option is that it makes it extremely easier to purchase exactly what you are looking for in a specific trade without needing to come up with additional capital just to end up with more than you actually need. For those who are interested in selling, weekly binary options make it easier to do so more regularly as opposed to having to wait a month or more between sales.

Weekly binary options trades are also worth considering in that they ultimately lead to lower costs for trades with larger spreads like calendar or diagonal spreads as you can sell weekly binary options against them in the interim. They also come in handy when it comes to higher volumes of trades overall, especially when it comes to hedging larger positions in risky markets. Likewise, if the market is range bound the weekly market will still be fruitful thanks to strategies like the iron condor or iron butterfly.

The biggest downside to weekly binary options is that you won't have much of a chance of things changing in your favor if you choose poorly from the start. Likewise, if you are looking to short the binary option in question then it is important to keep in mind that it would only take a relatively small overall move to push something into the money.

It is also important to keep in mind that these types of options require even more micromanaging than most which means that if you do not take the time to size up your trades properly as a means of guaranteeing profits you will find that you total trade balance starts to drop quite sharply. Along similar lines, the implied volatility for each trade is going to be higher than would otherwise be the case because of the shorten timeframe that you are dealing with. Near term options will always be subject to bigger swings as well.

As you will have less time with which to turn a profit when dealing with weekly binary options when you do make a move it is vital that your timing is as precise as possible as if you choose poorly then you can easily find yourself paying for something that will end up being worthless practically as soon as you put your money down. It is also important to consider how much risk the option offers as buying in bulk is always cheaper if you have the data to back it up.

Along similar lines, it is important to avoid naked puts or calls when trading in the weekly timeframe as these often end up with a lower probability of success overall. If you are quite specific when it comes to the directions of your chosen trades then a structured trade or a debit spread may be a better choice.

Selling weekly at a reliable pace for the long-term can lead to reliable profits when done correctly. It is likely to only work out if you strive to define your profits from the start which means you always need to know the odds on all of your current options to avoid selling yourself short by mistake. Selling weekly makes it easier to secure reliable profits while requiring extra margin to prevent unmitigated losses if you end up choosing poorly.

The most reliable type of trades to move forward with in this scenario it is important to look into trades with lots of implied volatility as it is more likely to work out in your favor in the long run due to the either/or nature of binary options. Spreads are another useful way to make money from the weekly market as the overall implied volatility will typically be higher when compared to the monthly variation which means the spread can help deal with an unexpected change in direction with the speed required to do something about it. Selling against a long option, meanwhile, will serve to decrease the amount of volatility in the transaction which means the ideal point to use the debt spread will be near the current price assuming the ratio of risk to reward is close to 1 to 1.

Intraday trading: While binary options are typically not considered when it comes to a successful day trading strategy, this new trend is quickly gaining steam as traders realize that many of the standard day trading techniques can be used when it comes to buying and selling binary options successfully.

When it comes to day trading options you will find there are some unique challenges than can be bested with the proper planning. The first issue you will need to be on the lookout for is the fact that price movement tends to decrease in value more significantly thanks to the time value that is associated with options that are only near the money when they are close to expiring. It is also important to keep in mind that while their inherent value may increase this may be countered by the loss incurred by the dropping time value.

The bid ask spread is often wider in these scenarios than would otherwise be the case due to the reduction in liquidity that is common within the options market. This will often vary by as much as half a point which can cut into profits if things start moving at the wrong time. Likewise, some options are naturally going to be a better fit for day trading than others. One of the most effective is the near month in the money option which is useful for those who enjoy trading in higher than average levels of liquidity. The premium for this type of option is often based more closely on the overall value because it will already be in the money by the time the expiration date draws near. When this happens the time value drain decreased significantly. This type of option tends to be the most effective in times of high volume which often results in a smaller gap between bid and ask price.

Chapter 8 - Technical Analysis and Its Basics

No matter the kind of vehicle you choose for your actions, there are some basics that you have to be familiar with. This fundamental knowledge is mostly connected to the behavior of the markets. If you learn how to recognize the way they behave, you will be able to anticipate the movement of the prices more accurately, thus make smarter decisions while trading. It can be interesting to note that regardless of the value that is traded on the market, some concepts can always apply to the prices and their way of performance on the market.

This can be explained by independent traders and investors being responsible for short-term price fluctuations. We can say that the price depends on the actions of the people who invest or trade values on the market and that prices react in a similar way when they are given similar input or stimuli. The study that is dedicated to researching the ways of price behavior is called technical analysis and understanding its basic is one of the most essential education points that you will need to be able to make correct financial decisions on the market.

The basics of Technical Analysis

Technical analysis represents a huge topic. If you decide to enter the market and become an investor, there is a high possibility that you will catch yourself coming back to studying and learning something new many times for as long as you intend to work as a trader. That is why every person knowledgeable in options trading would advise that a basic understanding of technical analysis is a very important step for every person involved in the market. However, you don't need to know everything about it right away. Since it is a large area of research, it is ok if for some aspects of your business you just research parts of the technical analysis that you are particularly interested in for that concrete project. For instance, the technical analysis offers more than a hundred indicators for analyzing the market. In reality, traders usually use three or four, mostly the most popular ones or just those that they were familiar within the first place.

If you don't limit yourself only to option trading but you do trading in general, you will realize that technical analysis can be applied to any financial instruments such as futures or stocks for example.

We can say that their basis is in psychology and human nature in general and how they behave in practice. For better understanding, we will overview some of the main topics in technical analysis. These topics will be:

Technical analysis' foundation; how to chart principles and trends; patterns in technical analysis; technical analysis through the movement of the averages, and Indicators in technical analysis.

Technical analysis' foundation

The main basis of the technical analysis is found in the term known as " market action". Market action represents a whole personal knowledge about the trading market, and it doesn't include information that you might obtain from an insider. It can be simply defined as a study that determines: "the way that the price moves over time". If possible, it also examines its volumes and how they change over time too.

Still, the fundamental concept of technical analysis is based on the premise that the behavior of the market is a reflection of everything that happened and will happen with the price at a certain moment. Many things can have an impact on the price, and the amount of the impact depends on the market in which the trade is made. That's where technical analysis comes in, it cuts across all of those possibilities and states that all the things that can be known about the price are basically already included in the price that we see at the moment we want to trade.

This means that you shouldn't worry too much about the things that influence the price, as according to this it is enough to follow how the price changes over time and you will get all your answers. At first, many people wondered if this kind of principle can work because it sounded rather easy. If you had any doubts, the answer was already proven and it says that yes, technical analysis is successful although this kind of definition doesn't seem that complicated.

However, there is one very important point coming out from all of this. Technical analysis doesn't guarantee the behavior of the price. It can tell you that the price will increase or decrease for a certain period, but that doesn't necessarily happen. It may or it may not. The reason for this is that regardless of the calculation that the market has to do something, it is impossible to be 100 percent sure that it will. The market has its own ways and eventually does what it wants. So what technical analysis does is that it gives you the indication that shows what will be the most probable outcome, which means that the only certainty that you get is to know if the law of probability is on your side or not.

You can do a large number of average trades and hopefully make some profit, but you should never invest an amount of money or some valuable goods such as your house or your car if you can't afford to lose it. It is not recommended especially if one successful trade makes you confident that just one is enough to be a good technical indicator for certain gain. This is one of the reasons why the first task of technical analysis is to improve your chance for success by analyzing the prices and the way they behave on the market.

The second reason for the analysis is the fact that prices almost always change using certain trends. For instance, if the price increases its trend will be to rise until there is something that disables it from further growth. In comparison, we can say that prices act like Newton's motion law, which says that: "a body in motion will stay in motion unless acted upon by an external force." Of course, to prove this to be true, it has to happen over time. If this wasn't the case the price charts represented in many analyses wouldn't be the way they are. They would be illustrated as a random movement of the prices. The third reason is that technical analysis supposes that history will, as always, repeat itself. If certain situations happened in the past, and you see them happening once again in the present than it is highly expected that the same thing will happen in the future too. Since people are not expected to change in this equation, the second logical conclusion would be that their results will be the same too. In a nutshell- this was a very foundation of technical analysis. Don't forget that one of the most efficient ways to become good in trading and to increase your chance to become a successful investor is to be able to use most of the things that this analysis can give you.

There are a few arguments that you can hear against the use of technical analysis. Still, the only proof that you really need is the fact that this analysis works and that at least it can improve your chances to get more percentages while trading. However, we will point out some of the attitudes toward technical analysis:

One of the traders said: "Charts only show what has happened in the past, how they can reveal what hasn't happened yet?" The answer to this is quite simple, there is evidence from earlier trades and those pieces of evidence are used in technical analysis with the premise that history will repeat itself. This way you can anticipate at least with some fair certainty what is the next thing that will happen with the price on the market. In comparison, it works in a similar way as the weather forecast, if they say that it will rain on the TV, you know that it might not rain even though they said it will, but you take your umbrella with you anyway. The same principle applies with the technical analysis and that is how you can predict the future by using the past events.

Another trader noted: "If the prices already incorporate everything there is to know, then any change in price can only come from new information that we don't know yet." This kind of idea doesn't only appear in trading options, it is present in all financial markets. It surfaces in many areas and even academics are still discussing it. Differently, from the opinion that is popular between the traders, this concept doesn't actually say that the price that is currently on the market is the correct one. It just states that it isn't possible to establish if that current price is too low or too high. That is why the smartest choice to deal with this concept is to prove in which way technical analysis really works. In the end, if everyone supported this kind of idea then we would have zero analysis and the price would be always the same. We can imply that technical analysis has self-fulfilling characteristics.

This means that if the majority of traders do the analysis and estimate that the price has to increase all of them would become buyers on the market, which would mean an increase in demand, thus price that went up. The same principle applies to the price that is supposed to go down. This is one more example in which technical analysis showed that it works. Of course, there can always be some doubts but does it really matter to prove why the price went in the direction that you thought it would? Additionally, if a large number of traders who are not well educated and they just want to make quick profit fail, it can be seen as a sort of evidence that the idea of having a massive amount of traders regardless of their knowledge and dedication is somehow wrong from the beginning.

How to chart principles and trends

After we have seen what the basic principles of the technical analysis are, it is time to see how the prices are charted or graphed and what those graphs mean. There is no way of escaping this even though some might find it unnecessary. You will be forced to see this kind of chart during your whole trading career. It is easier to understand these principles if you go slowly, step by step and try to remember how these principles work. There are few diverse types of the chart but all of them mostly use horizontal bottom and timescale as a vertical scale.

The price is usually up to the side, and for someone who is just starting, these charts are the only ones that you should be interested in. The vertical line or the timescale can be expressed in minutes, in days, or even weeks, so you will look at the one, which is suitable for your trading style. However, it is not unusual that you'd want to know what happens with the other time scales as long as they are around the values you chose. Experienced traders mostly look at the other time scales to get the bigger picture on what's happening on the market. Here, we will mention three kinds of charts and we will suppose that they all have the same time vertical line and that they are all in the same currency. Once that we accepted this hypothetical conditions we can say that here we will review the line chart, candlestick chart, and the bar chart.

In the first chart, we will talk about, the line chart is the one that has the least amount of information if we compare it to the other two. The only data you can find in this chart is the closing price's plots for certain periods and then these plots and periods are connected with the line. The line chart isn't used very often but it represents the basis for the next two- the candlestick and the bar chart. Even though all three show more or less the same information, traders prefer using the candlestick for instance, because according to them it is easier to understand it immediately when you see it, which is not the case with the rest of the mentioned charts. It is a way of recalling the definition of the "market action", which says that market action represents all we know about prices.

If you look at the chart that is known as the candlestick one, you will notice several vertical lines that are referred to like candles. These so-called candles can represent a four-hour chart for example, and the reason for that is the fact that in this period four plotted prices are different for every period in the chart. These prices are known as the highest price, the lowest price, the one that occurs at the beginning of the period (the opening price) and the one that is estimated to be at the end of the period or at the end of that trade (otherwise known as the closing price). Candlestick chart is actually a Japanese method for illustrating clearly this kind of information. However, this chart was used in the West for a few decades.

Before this chart appeared, the traders in the West used just the bar chart because it was the only one available at the time. The cleverness of the candlestick chart is shown through color change for example. The bar charts, on the other hand, use only thin lines, which we know as tics. These tics have their levels and they show closing prices and opening prices with these small tics. Contrarily, candles in the candlestick chart show you the difference in price by changing its color. The color depends on the value of the price for that day, and the change in color occurs with the price going up and down accordingly.

This way it is much easier to spot the changes in the chars. The common colors that are used in these charts are black and white. As you can already assume if the candle body is white the price will go up, and if it's black, the price is going down. Nowadays, technology is more improved, so there are options to put the colors that you like. The only criteria that matter is that you can immediately recognize if there are some changes in the market and if the price you were interested in ended uprising or falling.

When it comes to trends, the fundamental idea of trends is to indicate if the price will go up or down in general. Trends on the market are happening for about 40 percent of the time, on average. The rest of the time trends float around the same percentage and that kind of floating is known as moving "sideways", or range trading if you prefer. There are diverse strategies that can be useful if applied following the behavior of the market. For easier understanding, we will not go with the standard definitions of uptrends and downtrends. We will just say that the uptrend means that the price is going high and reaching even higher peaks but its point is low.

Contrarily, downtrend means that once that the points start going lower the next logical thing is that the price will tend to reach its lower peaks. As you can now assume, the trend doesn't mean that the prices will go only straight up or straight down. The prices don't do that, they wiggle around instead. Since trends are one of the most significant indicators of technical analysis, you must be very careful and try not to rely on the definition itself. Your point of view also has an influence on this matter. For example, let's say that you have a chart with a larger time frame in which we now see a simple uptrend. However, if you divide those uptrends into smaller periods you can see few smaller uptrends but this time they are interspersed with some small downtrends which are why you should observe your trends carefully especially the periods in which your trade should be over.

When a price acts reluctantly and it refuses to go beyond a certain level it means that we are talking about support and resistance. Support represents a level of price that is lower than the market one. If by any chance current price goes below that level it can happen that it will go back up or reverse in the process.

Resistance is a level of price that is higher than the level of the current price. This means that if the current price goes over this level there is a high probability that will go back down. Some traders describe the role of the support and resistance levels as a kind of magic. These levels act like borders and they are quite resistant.

Some of the basic points of these "borders" say that the more times that the price hits either the support or resistance level and bounces back, the more you should base your estimations on those reactions. Also, going back further in time and finding the similar or even the same levels means that these levels are even stronger, thus more reliable. If by some chance current price penetrates one of these two levels then they will just reverse their role. For example, if the price breaks the resistance then it is highly probable that when it starts going down it will stop at that level using resistance as its support.

Chapter 9 - Princing and volatility strategies

While the stock market has long term trends that investors rely on fairly well as the years and decades go by, over the short term the stock market is highly volatile. By that, we mean that prices are fluctuating up and down and doing so over short time periods. Volatility is something that long-term investors ignore. It's why you will hear people that promote conservative investment strategies suggesting that buyers use dollar cost averaging. What this does is it averages out the volatility in the market. That way you don't risk making the mistake of buying stocks when the price is a bit higher than it should be, because you'll average that out by buying shares when it's a bit lower than it should be.

In a sense, over the short term, the stock market can be considered as a chaotic system. So from one day to the next, unless there is something specific on offer, like Apple introducing a new gadget that investors are going to think will be a major hit, you can't be sure what the stock price is going to be tomorrow or the day after that. An increase on one day doesn't mean more increases are coming; it might be followed by a major dip the following day.

For example, at the time of writing, checking Apple's stock price, on the previous Friday it bottomed out at $196. Over the following days, it went up and down several times, and on the most recent close, it was $203. The movements over a short-term period appear random, and to a certain extent, they are. It's only over the long term that we see the actual direction that Apple is heading.

Of course, Apple is at the end of a ten-year run that began with the introduction of the iPhone and iPad. It's a reasonable bet that while it's a solid long-term investment, the stock probably isn't going to be moving enough for the purposes of making good profits over the short term from trades on call options (not too mention the per share price is relatively high).

The truth is volatility is actually a friend of the trader who buys call options. But it's a friend you have to be wary of because you can benefit from volatility while also getting in big trouble from it.

The reason stocks with more volatility are the friend of the options trader is that in part the options trader is playing a probability game. In other words, you're looking for stocks that have a chance of beating the strike price you need in order to make profits. A volatile stock that has large movements has a greater probability of not only passing your strike price but doing so in such a fashion that it far exceeds your strike price enabling you to make a large profit.

Of course, the alternative problem exists – that the stock price will suddenly drop. That is why care needs to be a part of your trader's toolkit. A stock with a high level of volatility is just as likely to suddenly drop in price as it is to skip right past your strike price.

Moreover, while you're a beginner and might get caught with your pants down, volatile stocks are going to attract experienced options traders. That means that the stock will be in high demand when it comes to options contracts. What happens when there is a high demand for something? The price shoots up. In the case of call options, that means the stock will come with a higher premium. You will need to take the higher premium into account when being able to exercise your options at the right time and make sure the price is high enough above your strike price that you don't end up losing money.

Traders take some time to examine the volatility of a given stock over the recent past, but they also look into what's known as implied volatility. This is a kind of weather forecast for stocks. It's an estimate of the future price movements of a stock, and it has a large influence on the pricing of options. Implied volatility is denoted by the Greek symbol σ, implied volatility increases in bear markets, and it actually decreases when investors are bullish. Implied volatility is a tool that can provide insight into the options future value.

For options traders, more volatility is a good thing. A stock that doesn't have much volatility is going to be a stable stock whose price isn't going to change very much over the lifetime of a contract. So while you may want to sell a covered call for a stock with low volatility, you're probably not going to want to buy one if you're buying call options because that means there will be a lower probability that the stock will change enough to exceed the strike price so you can earn a profit on a trade. Remember too that stocks that are very volatile will attract a lot of interest from options traders and command higher premiums. You will have to do some balancing in picking stocks that are of interest.

Being able to pick stocks that will have the right amount of volatility so that you can be sure of getting one that will earn profits on short term trades is something you're only going to get from experience. You should spend some time practicing before actually investing large amounts of money. That is, pick stocks you are interested in and make your bets but don't actually make the trades. Then follow them over the time period of the contract and see what happens. In the meantime, you can purchase safer call options, and so using this two-pronged approach gain experience that will lead to more surefire success down the road.

One thing that volatility means for everyone is that predicting the future is an impossible exercise. You're going to have some misses no matter how much knowledge and experience you gain. The only thing to aim for is to beat the market more often than you lose. The biggest mistake you can make is putting your life savings into a single stock that you think is a sure thing and then losing it all.

Options to pursue if your options aren't working

At this point, you may think that if the underlying stock for your option doesn't go anywhere or it tanks that you have no choice but to wait out the expiration date and count the money you spend on your premiums as a loss. That really isn't the case. The truth is, you can sell a call option you've purchased to other traders in the event its not working for you. Of course, you're not going to make a profit taking this approach in the vast majority of cases. But it will give you a chance to recoup some of your losses. If you have invested in a large number of call options for a specific stock and it's causing you problems, you need to recoup at least some of your losses may be more acute. Of course, the right course of action in these cases is rarely certain, especially if the expiration date for the contract is relatively far off in the future, which could mean that the stock has many chances to turn around and beat your strike price. Remember, in all bad scenarios actually buying the shares of stock is an option

– you're not required to do it. In all cases, the biggest loss you're facing is losing the entire premium. You'll also want to keep the following rule of thumb in mind at all times – the more time value an option has, the higher the price you can sell the option for. If there isn't much time value left, then you're probably going to have to sell the option at a discount. If there is a lot of time value, you may be able to recoup most of your losses on the premium.

Let's look at some specific scenarios

•   The stock is languishing. If the stock is losing time value (that is getting closer to the expiration date) and doesn't seem to be going anywhere, you can consider selling the call option in order to recoup some of your losses related to the premium. The more time value, the less likely it is that selling the option is a good idea. Of course, the less time value, the harder it's going to be to actually sell your option. Or put another way, in order to actually sell it you're going to have to take a lower price.

•   Suppose the stock isn't stagnant, but it's tanking. If there is a lot of time value left and there is some reason to believe that the company is going to make moves before the expiration date of your contract that will improve the fortunes of the stock when you can still profit from it, then you may want to ride out the downturn. This is a risky judgment call, and it's going to be impossible to know for sure what the right answer is, but you can make an educated guess. On the other hand, if the stock is tanking and there is no good news about the company on the horizon, you are pretty much facing the certainty that you're not going to be able to exercise your options to buy the shares. In that case, you should probably look at selling the option contract to someone more willing to take the risk. At least you can get some of the money back that you paid for the premium.

Now let's briefly consider the positive scenario. Buying options and then trading the stocks can feel like a roller coaster ride, and that rush is what attracts a lot of people to options trading besides the possibilities of making short term profits. Let's consider an example where the stock keeps rising in price? How long do you wait before selling?

There are two risks here. The first risk is that you're too anxious to sell and so do it at the first opportunity. That really isn't a huge downside; you're going to make some profits in that case. On the other hand, it's going to be disconcerting when you sit back and watch the stock continuing to rise. That said, this is better than some of the alternatives.

One of the alternatives is waiting too long to buy and sell the shares. You might wait and see the stock apparently reaching a peak, and then get a little greedy hoping that it's going to keep increasing so you can make even more profits. But then you keep waiting, and suddenly the stock starts dropping. Maybe you wait a little more hoping it's going to start rebounding and going up again, but it doesn't, and you're forced to buy and sell at a lower price than you could have gotten. Maybe it's even dropping enough so that you lose your opportunity altogether. A really volatile stock might suddenly crash, leaving you with a lost opportunity.

The reality is that like everything else involved in options trading since none of us can see the future it's going to be flat out impossible to know if you are making the right call every single time. Keep in mind that your goal is to make a profit on your trades. Don't get greedy about it, hoping for more riches than you actually see on the screen. In other words, the goal isn't to sell at maximum possible profits. Nobody knows what those are because it's going to be virtually impossible to predict what price the stock will peak at before the contract expires. Instead, you're going to want to focus on making an acceptable profit. Before you even buy your call options, you should sit down and figure out a reasonable range of values that define ahead of time what that acceptable profit level is. Then when the stock price hits your target range, you exercise your options and sell the shares. You take your profit and move on, going to the next trades.

That is not a guarantee that you're going to make money on every trade, but it's a more rules-based system that gets you into the mindset of trading based on objective facts rather than relying on unbridled emotions.

Also, remember that you can exercise the option to buy the shares, and then hold them until you think you've reached the right moment to sell. At other times, you may want to exercise the option to buy shares and hold in your portfolio as a long-term investment.

Bonus Chapter : - Think about choosing a broker

When it comes to selecting brokers, you have many options available. There are full service, discount, online, etc. Understanding the differences between them and selecting the ones best suited for your purposes is crucial if you wish to succeed. Another area that a lot of beginners ignore and then receive a rude lesson in is the regulations surrounding options trading.

There aren't too many rules to comply with, but they do have significant consequences for your capital and risk strategies. This chapter is going to fill you in on all the details.

Choosing a Broker

Generally speaking, there are two major varieties of brokers: Discount and full service. In fact, a lot of full-service brokers have discount arms these days so you will see some overlap. Full service refers to an organization where brokerage is just a part of a larger financial supermarket.

The broker might offer you other investment solutions, estate planning strategies, and so on. They'll also have an in house research wing which will send you reports to help you trade better. In addition to this, they'll also have phone support in case you have any questions or wish to place an order.

Once you develop a good relationship with them, a full-service broker will become a good organization to network. Every broker loves a profitable customer since it helps with marketing. A full-service broker will have good relationships in the industry and if you have specific needs, they can put you in touch with the right people.

The price of all this service is you paying higher commissions than average. It is up to you to see whether this is a good price for you to pay. As such, you don't need to signup with a full-service broker to trade successfully. Order matching is done electronically so it's not as if a person on the floor can get you a better price these days. Therefore, a full-service house is not going to give you better execution.

Discount brokers, on the other hand, are all about focus. They help you trade, and that is it. They will not provide advice, at least not intentionally from a business perspective, and phone ordering is nonexistent. That doesn't mean customer service is reduced. Far from it.

Commissions will be lower as well, far lower than what you can expect to pay at a full-service house. The downside of a discount brokerage is that you're not going to receive any special product recommendations or solutions outside of your speculative activities. A lot of people prefer to trade (using a separate account) with the broker they have their retirement accounts with so everything is kept in-house.

So which one should you choose? Well, if you aim to keep costs as low as possible, then select a discount broker. In fact, only in the case where you're keen on keeping things in one place should you choose a full-service broker. These days, there's no difference between the two options otherwise.

An exception here is if you have a large amount of capital, north of half a million dollars. In such cases, a full-service broker will be cheaper because of their volume-based commission offers. You'll pay the same rate or as close to what a discount broker would charge you, and you get all the additional services. Whatever additional amounts you need to invest can be handled by the firm through their wealth management line of business.

There are a few terms you must understand, no matter which broker you choose so let's look at these now.

Margin

Margin refers to the number of assets you currently hold in your account. Your assets are cash and positions. As the market value of your positions fluctuates, so does the amount of margin you have. Margin is an important concept to grasp since it is at the core of your risk management discipline.

When you open an account with your broker, you will have a choice to make. You can open either a cash or margin account. In order to trade options, you have to open a margin account. Briefly, a cash account does not include leverage within it, so all you can trade are stocks. There are no account minimums for a cash account, and even if they are, they're pretty minuscule.

A margin account, on the other hand, is subject to very different rules. First, the minimum balances for a margin account are higher. Most brokers will impose a $10,000 minimum, and some will even increase this amount based on your trading style. The account minimum doesn't achieve anything by itself, but it acts as a commitment of sorts for the broker.

The thinking is that with this much money on the line, the person trading is going to be a bit more serious about it and won't blow it away. If only it worked like that. Anyway, the minimum balance is a hard and fast rule. Another rule you should be aware of is the Pattern Day Trader (PDT) designation.

PDT is a rule that comes directly from the SEC. Anyone who executes four or more orders within five days is classified as a PDT ("Pattern Day Trader," 2019). One this tag is slapped onto you, your broker is going to ask you to post at least $25,000 in the margin as a minimum balance. Again, this minimum balance doesn't do anything but the SEC figures that if you do screw up, this gives you enough of a buffer.

Will the strategies in this book get you classified as a PDT? Well, this depends on you. Each strategy by itself plays out over a month or more so once you enter, all you need to do is monitor it and if you want, you can adjust it. However, if you're going to avoid the PDT, you're limited to entering just three positions per workweek.

My advice is to study the strategies and to start slowly. Trade just one instrument at first and see how it goes and then expand once you gain more confidence. At that point, you'll have enough experience to figure out how much capital you need. Remember that even exiting a position is considered a trade, so PDT doesn't refer just to trade entry.

Conclusion

Thank you for taking the time to read this little book about options. I hope that this has taken some of the mystery out of options and that you may feel more comfortable in pursuing a career trading them or just trading options on the side.

Options are often portrayed as being extremely risky, but they are only risky if you trade blind. In fact, options don't really carry that much. If you are foolish and let options that you buy head right into expiration without selling them off, or when a stock is in an obvious downward trend but you hold on to your call options bet that went bad, then I suppose that options are really risky. But for those that take the time to learn about it and study the concept carefully, trading options should not be that complicated or risky.

There are many different strategies that can be employed. Remember, however, that to use them you are going to have to get the appropriate trader level designation. Once you do, then you can use options to do amazing things that stock traders simply cannot do. Your friends with mutual funds will be grumbling when the stock market is crashing, but you will be smiling because you will be using the strategies outlined in this book in order to earn big profits from the downturn. Then when it reverses course you will return to your normal way of trading, and continue to make money.

Please don't stop with this book. You should continue studying and learning so that you can be a successful trader.

www.ingramcontent.com/pod-product-compliance
Lightning Source LLC
Chambersburg PA
CBHW050241220526
45465CB00002B/508